50 Ice Cream Recipes for Summer

By: Kelly Johnson

Table of Contents

- Classic Vanilla Bean Ice Cream
- Mango Sorbet
- Chocolate Hazelnut Gelato
- Lemon and Blueberry Ice Cream
- Strawberry Basil Ice Cream
- Coconut Milk Ice Cream
- Watermelon Sorbet
- Matcha Green Tea Ice Cream
- Peach and Cream Ice Cream
- Piña Colada Sorbet
- Salted Caramel Swirl Ice Cream
- Mint Chocolate Chip Ice Cream
- Raspberry Coconut Ice Cream
- Cherry Almond Ice Cream
- Lemon Curd Ice Cream
- Pistachio Ice Cream
- Brown Sugar Cinnamon Ice Cream
- Blackberry Yogurt Ice Cream
- Key Lime Pie Ice Cream
- Chocolate Peanut Butter Swirl Ice Cream
- S'mores Ice Cream
- Coconut and Lime Sorbet
- Coffee and Cream Ice Cream
- Strawberry Shortcake Ice Cream
- Mango Coconut Ice Cream
- Chocolate Covered Banana Ice Cream
- Blueberry Lemonade Sorbet
- Buttermilk Vanilla Bean Ice Cream
- Caramelized Banana Ice Cream
- Rum Raisin Ice Cream
- Raspberry Lime Sorbet
- Chocolate Cherry Chunk Ice Cream
- Apricot Almond Gelato
- Maple Pecan Ice Cream
- Lemon Lavender Ice Cream

- Chocolate Mint Chip Ice Cream
- Honey Almond Ice Cream
- Watermelon Mint Sorbet
- Cinnamon Roll Ice Cream
- Apple Cinnamon Ice Cream
- Nutella Swirl Ice Cream
- Tropical Fruit Ice Cream
- Almond Joy Ice Cream
- Pineapple Coconut Sorbet
- Sweet Corn and Honey Ice Cream
- Chocolate Marshmallow Ice Cream
- Orange Creamsicle Ice Cream
- Banana Foster Ice Cream
- Mixed Berry Sorbet
- Salted Chocolate Ice Cream

Classic Vanilla Bean Ice Cream

Ingredients:

- 2 cups heavy cream
- 1 cup whole milk
- 3/4 cup granulated sugar
- 1 vanilla bean, split and scraped
- 4 large egg yolks
- 1 tsp vanilla extract

Instructions:

1. **Heat the cream and milk**: In a saucepan, combine the heavy cream, whole milk, and half of the sugar. Split the vanilla bean, scrape the seeds, and add both the seeds and pod to the mixture. Heat over medium heat until just simmering.
2. **Whisk the egg yolks**: In a separate bowl, whisk the egg yolks with the remaining sugar until pale and smooth.
3. **Temper the eggs**: Gradually add the warm cream mixture to the egg yolks, whisking constantly to temper the eggs. Pour the mixture back into the saucepan.
4. **Cook the custard**: Cook over low heat, stirring constantly until the custard thickens and coats the back of a spoon, about 8-10 minutes. Remove from heat.
5. **Chill and churn**: Remove the vanilla pod, and stir in the vanilla extract. Let the custard cool to room temperature, then refrigerate for 4 hours or overnight. Once chilled, churn in an ice cream maker according to the manufacturer's instructions. Freeze until firm.

Mango Sorbet

Ingredients:

- 4 ripe mangoes, peeled and diced
- 3/4 cup sugar
- 1/2 cup water
- 1 tbsp fresh lime juice

Instructions:

1. **Prepare the syrup**: In a small saucepan, combine the sugar and water. Heat over medium heat, stirring until the sugar dissolves. Let cool.
2. **Puree the mangoes**: In a blender or food processor, puree the diced mangoes until smooth.
3. **Mix the ingredients**: Add the cooled syrup and lime juice to the mango puree. Blend until combined.
4. **Churn the sorbet**: Pour the mixture into an ice cream maker and churn according to the manufacturer's instructions. Freeze until firm.

Chocolate Hazelnut Gelato

Ingredients:

- 2 cups whole milk
- 1 cup heavy cream
- 1/2 cup sugar
- 1/2 cup hazelnut paste or Nutella
- 3 oz dark chocolate, chopped
- 4 large egg yolks
- 1 tsp vanilla extract

Instructions:

1. **Heat the milk and cream**: In a saucepan, combine the milk, cream, and half of the sugar. Heat over medium heat until it begins to simmer.
2. **Whisk the egg yolks**: In a separate bowl, whisk the egg yolks with the remaining sugar until pale and smooth.
3. **Temper the eggs**: Slowly add the hot milk mixture to the egg yolks, whisking constantly. Return the mixture to the saucepan and cook over low heat, stirring until it thickens and coats the back of a spoon.
4. **Add chocolate and hazelnut**: Remove from heat and stir in the chopped chocolate and hazelnut paste. Let the mixture cool completely, then refrigerate for 4 hours or overnight.
5. **Churn and freeze**: Once chilled, churn in an ice cream maker according to the manufacturer's instructions. Freeze until firm.

Lemon and Blueberry Ice Cream

Ingredients:

- 2 cups heavy cream
- 1 cup whole milk
- 3/4 cup sugar
- 1 tbsp lemon zest
- 1/4 cup lemon juice
- 1 cup blueberries
- 1/2 cup sugar (for the blueberries)

Instructions:

1. **Cook the blueberries**: In a small saucepan, combine the blueberries and sugar. Heat over medium heat until the blueberries break down and the mixture becomes syrupy, about 5-7 minutes. Let it cool.
2. **Make the base**: In a separate bowl, whisk together the heavy cream, whole milk, sugar, lemon zest, and lemon juice.
3. **Combine the blueberry mixture**: Blend the cooked blueberries into the cream mixture until smooth.
4. **Churn the ice cream**: Pour the mixture into an ice cream maker and churn according to the manufacturer's instructions. Freeze until firm.

Strawberry Basil Ice Cream

Ingredients:

- 2 cups fresh strawberries, hulled and chopped
- 1 cup heavy cream
- 1 cup whole milk
- 3/4 cup sugar
- 1 tbsp lemon juice
- 1/4 cup fresh basil, chopped

Instructions:

1. **Prepare the strawberries**: Blend the strawberries, lemon juice, and sugar until smooth. Let it sit for about 30 minutes to macerate.
2. **Infuse the cream**: Heat the heavy cream and whole milk in a saucepan over medium heat until simmering. Remove from heat and add the chopped basil. Let it steep for 10 minutes, then strain out the basil.
3. **Combine the mixture**: Stir the strawberry puree into the infused cream. Let the mixture cool to room temperature, then refrigerate for 4 hours or overnight.
4. **Churn and freeze**: Once chilled, churn in an ice cream maker according to the manufacturer's instructions. Freeze until firm.

Coconut Milk Ice Cream

Ingredients:

- 2 cans full-fat coconut milk
- 1/2 cup sugar
- 1 tsp vanilla extract
- Pinch of salt

Instructions:

1. **Mix the ingredients**: In a large bowl, whisk together the coconut milk, sugar, vanilla extract, and salt until the sugar dissolves.
2. **Churn the ice cream**: Pour the mixture into an ice cream maker and churn according to the manufacturer's instructions. Freeze until firm.

Watermelon Sorbet

Ingredients:

- 4 cups watermelon, cubed and seeded
- 1/2 cup sugar
- 1/4 cup fresh lime juice

Instructions:

1. **Prepare the watermelon**: Blend the watermelon cubes until smooth.
2. **Make the syrup**: In a small saucepan, combine the sugar and lime juice. Heat over medium heat until the sugar dissolves, then let it cool.
3. **Mix the ingredients**: Combine the watermelon puree with the syrup and stir well.
4. **Churn the sorbet**: Pour the mixture into an ice cream maker and churn according to the manufacturer's instructions. Freeze until firm.

Matcha Green Tea Ice Cream

Ingredients:

- 2 cups heavy cream
- 1 cup whole milk
- 3/4 cup sugar
- 2 tbsp matcha powder
- 4 large egg yolks

Instructions:

1. **Heat the milk and cream**: In a saucepan, combine the heavy cream and whole milk. Heat over medium heat until it begins to simmer.
2. **Whisk the egg yolks**: In a separate bowl, whisk the egg yolks with sugar and matcha powder until smooth.
3. **Temper the eggs**: Gradually add the hot milk mixture to the egg yolks, whisking constantly. Return the mixture to the saucepan and cook over low heat until it thickens.
4. **Chill and churn**: Let the mixture cool to room temperature, then refrigerate for 4 hours or overnight. Once chilled, churn in an ice cream maker according to the manufacturer's instructions. Freeze until firm.

Peach and Cream Ice Cream

Ingredients:

- 4 ripe peaches, peeled and diced
- 2 cups heavy cream
- 1 cup whole milk
- 3/4 cup sugar
- 1 tsp vanilla extract
- 1 tbsp lemon juice

Instructions:

1. **Prepare the peaches**: In a blender or food processor, puree the peaches with lemon juice and 1/4 cup of the sugar. Set aside.
2. **Make the base**: In a saucepan, heat the heavy cream, whole milk, and remaining sugar over medium heat, stirring until the sugar dissolves.
3. **Combine**: Remove the milk mixture from the heat and stir in the vanilla extract. Once the mixture has cooled to room temperature, stir in the peach puree.
4. **Churn the ice cream**: Pour the mixture into an ice cream maker and churn according to the manufacturer's instructions. Freeze until firm.

Piña Colada Sorbet

Ingredients:

- 2 cups fresh pineapple, chopped
- 1 cup coconut milk
- 1/2 cup sugar
- 1/4 cup fresh lime juice
- 1 tbsp dark rum (optional)

Instructions:

1. **Blend the ingredients**: Combine the pineapple, coconut milk, sugar, lime juice, and rum (if using) in a blender or food processor. Blend until smooth.
2. **Chill**: Pour the mixture into a bowl and refrigerate for about an hour to chill.
3. **Churn**: Once chilled, pour the mixture into an ice cream maker and churn according to the manufacturer's instructions. Freeze until firm.

Salted Caramel Swirl Ice Cream

Ingredients:

- 2 cups heavy cream
- 1 cup whole milk
- 3/4 cup sugar
- 1 tsp vanilla extract
- 1/2 cup salted caramel sauce (store-bought or homemade)

Instructions:

1. **Make the base**: In a saucepan, combine the heavy cream, whole milk, and sugar. Heat over medium heat, stirring occasionally, until the sugar dissolves.
2. **Add vanilla**: Remove from heat and stir in the vanilla extract. Let the mixture cool to room temperature.
3. **Churn the ice cream**: Pour the mixture into an ice cream maker and churn according to the manufacturer's instructions.
4. **Swirl in the caramel**: Once the ice cream is churned, fold in the salted caramel sauce to create a swirl. Freeze until firm.

Mint Chocolate Chip Ice Cream

Ingredients:

- 2 cups heavy cream
- 1 cup whole milk
- 3/4 cup sugar
- 1 tsp peppermint extract
- 1/2 cup mini chocolate chips
- 4 large egg yolks

Instructions:

1. **Make the custard base**: In a saucepan, combine the heavy cream, whole milk, and half of the sugar. Heat over medium heat until it begins to simmer.
2. **Whisk the egg yolks**: In a separate bowl, whisk the egg yolks with the remaining sugar until pale and smooth.
3. **Temper the eggs**: Slowly add the hot milk mixture to the egg yolks, whisking constantly. Return the mixture to the saucepan and cook over low heat until it thickens.
4. **Chill and churn**: Remove from heat and stir in the peppermint extract. Let the mixture cool to room temperature, then refrigerate for 4 hours or overnight. Once chilled, churn in an ice cream maker according to the manufacturer's instructions. Stir in the chocolate chips during the last few minutes of churning. Freeze until firm.

Raspberry Coconut Ice Cream

Ingredients:

- 2 cups heavy cream
- 1 cup whole milk
- 1/2 cup sugar
- 1 cup fresh raspberries
- 1/2 cup shredded coconut
- 1 tsp vanilla extract

Instructions:

1. **Prepare the raspberries**: Blend the raspberries with 1/4 cup of the sugar until smooth.
2. **Make the base**: In a saucepan, combine the heavy cream, whole milk, and the remaining sugar. Heat over medium heat until the sugar dissolves.
3. **Combine**: Remove from heat and stir in the vanilla extract. Add the raspberry puree and shredded coconut to the mixture.
4. **Churn and freeze**: Once the mixture is cool, pour it into an ice cream maker and churn according to the manufacturer's instructions. Freeze until firm.

Cherry Almond Ice Cream

Ingredients:

- 2 cups heavy cream
- 1 cup whole milk
- 3/4 cup sugar
- 1 cup fresh cherries, pitted and chopped
- 1/4 cup sliced almonds
- 1 tsp almond extract

Instructions:

1. **Prepare the cherries**: In a saucepan, cook the chopped cherries with 2 tablespoons of sugar over medium heat for about 5 minutes, until softened. Set aside to cool.
2. **Make the base**: In a separate saucepan, combine the heavy cream, whole milk, and the remaining sugar. Heat over medium heat until the sugar dissolves.
3. **Combine**: Remove from heat and stir in the almond extract. Once the mixture has cooled to room temperature, stir in the cherry mixture and sliced almonds.
4. **Churn the ice cream**: Pour the mixture into an ice cream maker and churn according to the manufacturer's instructions. Freeze until firm.

Lemon Curd Ice Cream

Ingredients:

- 1 cup lemon curd (store-bought or homemade)
- 2 cups heavy cream
- 1 cup whole milk
- 1/2 cup sugar

Instructions:

1. **Make the base**: In a saucepan, combine the heavy cream, whole milk, and sugar. Heat over medium heat until the sugar dissolves.
2. **Add the lemon curd**: Remove from heat and stir in the lemon curd until smooth.
3. **Churn the ice cream**: Let the mixture cool to room temperature, then refrigerate for 4 hours or overnight. Once chilled, churn in an ice cream maker according to the manufacturer's instructions. Freeze until firm.

Pistachio Ice Cream

Ingredients:

- 2 cups heavy cream
- 1 cup whole milk
- 3/4 cup sugar
- 1/2 cup shelled pistachios
- 1 tsp vanilla extract
- 4 large egg yolks

Instructions:

1. **Prepare the pistachios**: Blend the pistachios in a food processor until finely ground, then set aside.
2. **Make the custard**: In a saucepan, combine the heavy cream, whole milk, and half of the sugar. Heat over medium heat until it begins to simmer.
3. **Whisk the egg yolks**: In a separate bowl, whisk the egg yolks with the remaining sugar until pale and smooth.
4. **Temper the eggs**: Slowly add the hot cream mixture to the egg yolks, whisking constantly. Return the mixture to the saucepan and cook over low heat until it thickens.
5. **Churn the ice cream**: Remove from heat and stir in the ground pistachios and vanilla extract. Let the mixture cool, then refrigerate for 4 hours or overnight. Once chilled, churn in an ice cream maker according to the manufacturer's instructions. Freeze until firm.

Brown Sugar Cinnamon Ice Cream

Ingredients:

- 2 cups heavy cream
- 1 cup whole milk
- 3/4 cup brown sugar
- 1 tsp ground cinnamon
- 1 tsp vanilla extract
- 1/4 tsp salt

Instructions:

1. **Make the base**: In a saucepan, combine the heavy cream, whole milk, brown sugar, cinnamon, and salt. Heat over medium heat, stirring occasionally until the sugar dissolves and the mixture is hot but not boiling.
2. **Cool the mixture**: Remove from heat and stir in the vanilla extract. Allow the mixture to cool to room temperature, then refrigerate for 4 hours or overnight.
3. **Churn the ice cream**: Once chilled, pour the mixture into an ice cream maker and churn according to the manufacturer's instructions. Freeze until firm.

Blackberry Yogurt Ice Cream

Ingredients:

- 2 cups fresh blackberries
- 1 cup whole milk
- 1 cup plain yogurt
- 1 cup heavy cream
- 3/4 cup sugar
- 1 tsp vanilla extract

Instructions:

1. **Prepare the blackberries**: In a blender, puree the blackberries with 1/4 cup of the sugar. Set aside.
2. **Make the base**: In a mixing bowl, combine the whole milk, yogurt, heavy cream, and the remaining sugar. Stir until the sugar dissolves.
3. **Combine**: Stir in the blackberry puree and vanilla extract. Refrigerate the mixture for 4 hours or overnight.
4. **Churn**: Once chilled, churn the mixture in an ice cream maker according to the manufacturer's instructions. Freeze until firm.

Key Lime Pie Ice Cream

Ingredients:

- 1 1/2 cups heavy cream
- 1 cup whole milk
- 3/4 cup sugar
- 1/2 cup key lime juice
- 1 tsp vanilla extract
- 1/2 cup crushed graham crackers

Instructions:

1. **Make the base**: In a saucepan, combine the heavy cream, whole milk, and sugar. Heat over medium heat until the sugar dissolves and the mixture is warm.
2. **Add lime juice**: Remove from heat and stir in the key lime juice and vanilla extract. Allow to cool to room temperature, then refrigerate for 4 hours or overnight.
3. **Churn**: Once chilled, churn the mixture in an ice cream maker according to the manufacturer's instructions.
4. **Add graham crackers**: During the last few minutes of churning, add the crushed graham crackers. Freeze until firm.

Chocolate Peanut Butter Swirl Ice Cream

Ingredients:

- 2 cups heavy cream
- 1 cup whole milk
- 3/4 cup sugar
- 1/2 cup creamy peanut butter
- 1/2 cup chocolate sauce
- 1 tsp vanilla extract

Instructions:

1. **Make the base**: In a saucepan, combine the heavy cream, whole milk, and sugar. Heat over medium heat until the sugar dissolves.
2. **Cool the mixture**: Remove from heat and stir in the vanilla extract. Allow the mixture to cool to room temperature, then refrigerate for 4 hours or overnight.
3. **Churn**: Once chilled, churn the mixture in an ice cream maker according to the manufacturer's instructions.
4. **Swirl in peanut butter and chocolate**: After churning, swirl in the peanut butter and chocolate sauce. Freeze until firm.

S'mores Ice Cream

Ingredients:

- 2 cups heavy cream
- 1 cup whole milk
- 3/4 cup sugar
- 1 tsp vanilla extract
- 1/2 cup graham cracker crumbs
- 1/2 cup mini marshmallows
- 1/4 cup chocolate chips

Instructions:

1. **Make the base**: In a saucepan, combine the heavy cream, whole milk, and sugar. Heat over medium heat, stirring until the sugar dissolves.
2. **Cool the mixture**: Remove from heat and stir in the vanilla extract. Allow the mixture to cool to room temperature, then refrigerate for 4 hours or overnight.
3. **Churn**: Once chilled, churn the mixture in an ice cream maker according to the manufacturer's instructions.
4. **Add marshmallows and graham crackers**: After churning, fold in the graham cracker crumbs, mini marshmallows, and chocolate chips. Freeze until firm.

Coconut and Lime Sorbet

Ingredients:

- 1 1/2 cups coconut milk
- 1/2 cup lime juice
- 3/4 cup sugar
- 1 cup water

Instructions:

1. **Make the base**: In a saucepan, combine the coconut milk, lime juice, sugar, and water. Heat over medium heat, stirring occasionally until the sugar dissolves.
2. **Cool the mixture**: Remove from heat and allow the mixture to cool to room temperature. Refrigerate for 4 hours or overnight.
3. **Churn**: Once chilled, pour the mixture into an ice cream maker and churn according to the manufacturer's instructions. Freeze until firm.

Coffee and Cream Ice Cream

Ingredients:

- 2 cups heavy cream
- 1 cup whole milk
- 1/2 cup sugar
- 2 tbsp instant coffee or espresso powder
- 1 tsp vanilla extract

Instructions:

1. **Dissolve the coffee**: In a saucepan, combine the sugar and milk, and heat over medium heat, stirring until the sugar dissolves. Add the coffee powder and stir until completely dissolved.
2. **Make the base**: Remove from heat and stir in the heavy cream and vanilla extract. Let the mixture cool to room temperature, then refrigerate for 4 hours or overnight.
3. **Churn**: Once chilled, churn the mixture in an ice cream maker according to the manufacturer's instructions. Freeze until firm.

Strawberry Shortcake Ice Cream

Ingredients:

- 2 cups fresh strawberries, chopped
- 1 cup heavy cream
- 1 cup whole milk
- 3/4 cup sugar
- 1 tsp vanilla extract
- 1/2 cup crushed shortbread cookies

Instructions:

1. **Prepare the strawberries**: In a blender or food processor, puree the strawberries with 1/4 cup of sugar until smooth. Set aside.
2. **Make the base**: In a mixing bowl, combine the heavy cream, whole milk, and remaining sugar. Stir until the sugar dissolves.
3. **Combine**: Stir in the strawberry puree and vanilla extract.
4. **Churn**: Pour the mixture into an ice cream maker and churn according to the manufacturer's instructions. Once the ice cream is churned, fold in the crushed shortbread cookies. Freeze until firm.

Mango Coconut Ice Cream

Ingredients:

- 2 cups fresh mango puree
- 1 cup coconut milk
- 1 cup heavy cream
- 3/4 cup sugar
- 1 tsp vanilla extract
- 1/4 cup shredded coconut (optional)

Instructions:

1. **Prepare the mango puree**: In a blender, puree fresh mango until smooth.
2. **Make the base**: In a bowl, combine coconut milk, heavy cream, sugar, and vanilla extract. Stir until the sugar dissolves.
3. **Combine**: Add the mango puree to the cream mixture and mix well.
4. **Churn**: Pour the mixture into an ice cream maker and churn according to the manufacturer's instructions.
5. **Add shredded coconut**: During the last few minutes of churning, add shredded coconut if desired. Freeze until firm.

Chocolate Covered Banana Ice Cream

Ingredients:

- 2 ripe bananas, mashed
- 1 cup heavy cream
- 1/2 cup milk
- 1/4 cup sugar
- 1/2 tsp vanilla extract
- 1/4 cup mini chocolate chips
- 1/4 cup chocolate sauce

Instructions:

1. **Prepare the base**: In a bowl, mix the mashed bananas, heavy cream, milk, sugar, and vanilla extract until smooth.
2. **Churn**: Pour the mixture into an ice cream maker and churn according to the manufacturer's instructions.
3. **Add chocolate chips**: During the last few minutes of churning, add mini chocolate chips.
4. **Swirl with chocolate sauce**: Once the ice cream is churned, swirl in the chocolate sauce for that chocolate-covered banana effect. Freeze until firm.

Blueberry Lemonade Sorbet

Ingredients:

- 2 cups fresh blueberries
- 1/2 cup lemon juice
- 3/4 cup sugar
- 1 cup water
- Zest of 1 lemon

Instructions:

1. **Make the syrup**: In a saucepan, combine sugar and water. Heat over medium heat, stirring until sugar dissolves. Remove from heat and cool.
2. **Prepare the blueberries**: In a blender, puree fresh blueberries and lemon juice until smooth.
3. **Combine**: Stir the blueberry puree, lemon zest, and sugar syrup together. Refrigerate for 2 hours.
4. **Churn**: Pour the mixture into an ice cream maker and churn according to the manufacturer's instructions. Freeze until firm.

Buttermilk Vanilla Bean Ice Cream

Ingredients:

- 2 cups heavy cream
- 1 cup buttermilk
- 1 cup whole milk
- 3/4 cup sugar
- 1 vanilla bean (split and scraped)

Instructions:

1. **Prepare the base**: In a saucepan, heat the heavy cream, whole milk, and sugar over medium heat, stirring until the sugar dissolves.
2. **Add vanilla**: Once the mixture is warm, scrape the seeds from the vanilla bean and add both the seeds and pod to the saucepan. Let it steep for 10 minutes.
3. **Combine with buttermilk**: Remove from heat, discard the vanilla pod, and stir in the buttermilk.
4. **Cool and churn**: Allow the mixture to cool to room temperature, then refrigerate for 4 hours. Once chilled, churn in an ice cream maker according to the manufacturer's instructions. Freeze until firm.

Caramelized Banana Ice Cream

Ingredients:

- 3 ripe bananas, sliced
- 1/4 cup brown sugar
- 1 cup heavy cream
- 1 cup whole milk
- 3/4 cup sugar
- 1 tsp vanilla extract

Instructions:

1. **Caramelize the bananas**: In a skillet, cook the banana slices with brown sugar over medium heat until caramelized (about 5-7 minutes). Let them cool slightly.
2. **Make the base**: In a bowl, combine heavy cream, whole milk, sugar, and vanilla extract. Stir until the sugar dissolves.
3. **Blend with bananas**: Blend the caramelized bananas into the cream mixture until smooth.
4. **Churn**: Pour the mixture into an ice cream maker and churn according to the manufacturer's instructions. Freeze until firm.

Rum Raisin Ice Cream

Ingredients:

- 1 cup raisins
- 1/4 cup dark rum
- 2 cups heavy cream
- 1 cup whole milk
- 3/4 cup sugar
- 1 tsp vanilla extract

Instructions:

1. **Soak the raisins**: Soak the raisins in dark rum for at least 2 hours or overnight.
2. **Make the base**: In a bowl, combine heavy cream, whole milk, sugar, and vanilla extract. Stir until the sugar dissolves.
3. **Churn**: Pour the mixture into an ice cream maker and churn according to the manufacturer's instructions.
4. **Add raisins**: During the last few minutes of churning, add the rum-soaked raisins. Freeze until firm.

Raspberry Lime Sorbet

Ingredients:

- 2 cups fresh raspberries
- 1/2 cup lime juice
- 3/4 cup sugar
- 1 cup water

Instructions:

1. **Make the syrup**: In a saucepan, combine sugar and water. Heat over medium heat, stirring until sugar dissolves. Remove from heat and cool.
2. **Prepare the raspberries**: In a blender, puree the raspberries and lime juice until smooth.
3. **Combine**: Stir the raspberry puree and sugar syrup together. Refrigerate for 2 hours.
4. **Churn**: Pour the mixture into an ice cream maker and churn according to the manufacturer's instructions. Freeze until firm.

Chocolate Cherry Chunk Ice Cream

Ingredients:

- 2 cups heavy cream
- 1 cup whole milk
- 3/4 cup sugar
- 1/2 cup cocoa powder
- 1 tsp vanilla extract
- 1 cup cherries, pitted and chopped
- 1/4 cup chocolate chunks

Instructions:

1. **Make the base**: In a saucepan, combine heavy cream, whole milk, sugar, and cocoa powder. Heat over medium heat, stirring until the sugar dissolves and the cocoa is fully incorporated.
2. **Cool the mixture**: Remove from heat and stir in vanilla extract. Let the mixture cool to room temperature, then refrigerate for 4 hours or overnight.
3. **Churn**: Once chilled, churn the mixture in an ice cream maker according to the manufacturer's instructions.
4. **Add cherries and chocolate**: During the last few minutes of churning, add the chopped cherries and chocolate chunks. Freeze until firm.

Apricot Almond Gelato

Ingredients:

- 2 cups fresh apricots, peeled and chopped
- 1 cup whole milk
- 1 cup heavy cream
- 3/4 cup sugar
- 1/4 cup chopped almonds (toasted)
- 1 tsp almond extract
- 1 tbsp lemon juice

Instructions:

1. **Prepare the apricots**: In a saucepan, cook apricots and sugar over medium heat until soft (about 5-7 minutes). Let cool and puree in a blender with lemon juice until smooth.
2. **Make the base**: In a bowl, combine the milk, heavy cream, and almond extract. Stir until sugar dissolves.
3. **Combine**: Add the apricot puree to the milk mixture and stir well.
4. **Churn**: Pour the mixture into an ice cream maker and churn according to the manufacturer's instructions.
5. **Add toasted almonds**: During the last few minutes of churning, add the toasted almonds. Freeze until firm.

Maple Pecan Ice Cream

Ingredients:

- 1 cup maple syrup
- 2 cups heavy cream
- 1 cup whole milk
- 3/4 cup sugar
- 1 tsp vanilla extract
- 1 cup toasted pecans, chopped

Instructions:

1. **Prepare the base**: In a saucepan, combine maple syrup, heavy cream, whole milk, and sugar. Heat over medium heat, stirring until sugar dissolves. Remove from heat and stir in vanilla extract.
2. **Chill**: Let the mixture cool to room temperature, then refrigerate for 4 hours or overnight.
3. **Churn**: Pour the mixture into an ice cream maker and churn according to the manufacturer's instructions.
4. **Add pecans**: During the last few minutes of churning, add the toasted pecans. Freeze until firm.

Lemon Lavender Ice Cream

Ingredients:

- 1 1/2 cups heavy cream
- 1 cup whole milk
- 3/4 cup sugar
- Zest of 2 lemons
- 1 tbsp dried lavender buds
- 1 tsp lemon juice
- 1 tsp vanilla extract

Instructions:

1. **Infuse the cream**: In a saucepan, heat the cream and milk over medium heat. Add the lavender buds and lemon zest and let steep for 10 minutes. Strain the mixture and discard the lavender.
2. **Make the base**: In a bowl, whisk together sugar, lemon juice, and vanilla extract with the infused cream mixture.
3. **Chill**: Refrigerate the mixture for at least 4 hours or overnight.
4. **Churn**: Pour the mixture into an ice cream maker and churn according to the manufacturer's instructions. Freeze until firm.

Chocolate Mint Chip Ice Cream

Ingredients:

- 2 cups heavy cream
- 1 cup whole milk
- 3/4 cup sugar
- 1/2 cup unsweetened cocoa powder
- 1 tsp peppermint extract
- 1/2 cup mini chocolate chips

Instructions:

1. **Make the chocolate base**: In a saucepan, combine the heavy cream, whole milk, sugar, and cocoa powder. Heat over medium heat, stirring until the sugar dissolves and cocoa is fully incorporated. Remove from heat and stir in peppermint extract.
2. **Chill**: Let the mixture cool to room temperature, then refrigerate for 4 hours or overnight.
3. **Churn**: Once chilled, churn the mixture in an ice cream maker according to the manufacturer's instructions.
4. **Add chocolate chips**: During the last few minutes of churning, add the mini chocolate chips. Freeze until firm.

Honey Almond Ice Cream

Ingredients:

- 2 cups heavy cream
- 1 cup whole milk
- 1/2 cup honey
- 1/4 cup sugar
- 1 tsp vanilla extract
- 1/2 cup chopped toasted almonds

Instructions:

1. **Make the base**: In a bowl, combine heavy cream, whole milk, honey, sugar, and vanilla extract. Stir until sugar dissolves.
2. **Chill**: Refrigerate the mixture for 4 hours or overnight.
3. **Churn**: Once chilled, churn the mixture in an ice cream maker according to the manufacturer's instructions.
4. **Add almonds**: During the last few minutes of churning, add the toasted almonds. Freeze until firm.

Watermelon Mint Sorbet

Ingredients:

- 4 cups fresh watermelon, cubed and seeds removed
- 1/2 cup fresh mint leaves
- 3/4 cup sugar
- 1/4 cup lime juice

Instructions:

1. **Blend the watermelon**: In a blender, puree the watermelon until smooth. Strain through a fine mesh sieve to remove excess pulp.
2. **Prepare the syrup**: In a saucepan, combine sugar and 1/2 cup water. Heat over medium heat until sugar dissolves. Let cool.
3. **Combine**: Stir the sugar syrup and lime juice into the watermelon puree.
4. **Churn**: Pour the mixture into an ice cream maker and churn according to the manufacturer's instructions.
5. **Add mint**: Chop the mint leaves finely and stir into the sorbet after churning. Freeze until firm.

Cinnamon Roll Ice Cream

Ingredients:

- 2 cups heavy cream
- 1 cup whole milk
- 3/4 cup sugar
- 1 tsp vanilla extract
- 1 tbsp ground cinnamon
- 1/2 cup cinnamon roll dough, cubed and baked
- 1/2 cup caramel sauce (optional)

Instructions:

1. **Make the base**: In a bowl, combine heavy cream, whole milk, sugar, cinnamon, and vanilla extract. Stir until sugar dissolves.
2. **Chill**: Refrigerate the mixture for 4 hours or overnight.
3. **Churn**: Once chilled, churn the mixture in an ice cream maker according to the manufacturer's instructions.
4. **Add cinnamon rolls**: During the last few minutes of churning, add the cubed cinnamon rolls. Optionally, swirl in caramel sauce. Freeze until firm.

Apple Cinnamon Ice Cream

Ingredients:

- 2 cups heavy cream
- 1 cup whole milk
- 1 cup applesauce
- 3/4 cup sugar
- 1 tsp ground cinnamon
- 1/2 cup chopped apples (cooked or raw)

Instructions:

1. **Prepare the base**: In a bowl, combine heavy cream, whole milk, applesauce, sugar, and cinnamon. Stir until sugar dissolves.
2. **Chill**: Refrigerate the mixture for 4 hours or overnight.
3. **Churn**: Once chilled, churn the mixture in an ice cream maker according to the manufacturer's instructions.
4. **Add apples**: During the last few minutes of churning, add the chopped apples. Freeze until firm.

Nutella Swirl Ice Cream

Ingredients:

- 2 cups heavy cream
- 1 cup whole milk
- 3/4 cup sugar
- 1/2 cup Nutella
- 1 tsp vanilla extract

Instructions:

1. **Make the base**: In a bowl, combine heavy cream, whole milk, sugar, and vanilla extract. Stir until sugar dissolves.
2. **Chill**: Refrigerate the mixture for at least 4 hours or overnight.
3. **Churn**: Once chilled, churn the mixture in an ice cream maker according to the manufacturer's instructions.
4. **Swirl Nutella**: During the last few minutes of churning, drop spoonfuls of Nutella into the ice cream and swirl it gently to create ribbons of Nutella throughout the ice cream. Freeze until firm.

Tropical Fruit Ice Cream

Ingredients:

- 1 cup mango, peeled and chopped
- 1 cup pineapple, peeled and chopped
- 1 cup coconut milk
- 1 cup heavy cream
- 1/2 cup sugar
- 1 tbsp lime juice

Instructions:

1. **Prepare the fruit**: Puree the mango and pineapple together in a blender or food processor until smooth. If needed, strain the mixture to remove excess fiber.
2. **Make the base**: In a bowl, combine coconut milk, heavy cream, sugar, and lime juice. Stir until sugar dissolves.
3. **Combine**: Add the fruit puree to the coconut milk mixture and stir until well combined.
4. **Churn**: Pour the mixture into an ice cream maker and churn according to the manufacturer's instructions. Freeze until firm.

Almond Joy Ice Cream

Ingredients:

- 2 cups heavy cream
- 1 cup whole milk
- 3/4 cup sugar
- 1/2 cup shredded coconut
- 1/2 cup chopped almonds
- 1/2 cup chocolate chips
- 1 tsp vanilla extract

Instructions:

1. **Make the base**: In a bowl, combine heavy cream, whole milk, sugar, and vanilla extract. Stir until sugar dissolves.
2. **Chill**: Refrigerate the mixture for at least 4 hours or overnight.
3. **Churn**: Once chilled, churn the mixture in an ice cream maker according to the manufacturer's instructions.
4. **Add mix-ins**: During the last few minutes of churning, add the shredded coconut, chopped almonds, and chocolate chips. Freeze until firm.

Pineapple Coconut Sorbet

Ingredients:

- 4 cups fresh pineapple, peeled and chopped
- 1 cup coconut water
- 1/4 cup sugar
- 1 tbsp lime juice

Instructions:

1. **Puree the pineapple**: In a blender, puree the pineapple until smooth. Strain the mixture to remove any pulp if desired.
2. **Make the syrup**: In a saucepan, combine sugar and coconut water. Heat over medium heat until sugar dissolves. Let cool.
3. **Combine**: Stir the pineapple puree and lime juice into the cooled coconut water syrup.
4. **Churn**: Pour the mixture into an ice cream maker and churn according to the manufacturer's instructions. Freeze until firm.

Sweet Corn and Honey Ice Cream

Ingredients:

- 2 cups heavy cream
- 1 cup whole milk
- 1 cup sweet corn kernels (fresh or frozen)
- 1/2 cup honey
- 1/4 cup sugar
- 1 tsp vanilla extract

Instructions:

1. **Infuse the cream**: In a saucepan, heat the heavy cream and milk over medium heat. Add the corn kernels and simmer for 10-15 minutes. Let cool slightly, then strain the mixture, reserving the liquid and discarding the corn.
2. **Make the base**: In a bowl, combine the infused cream and milk mixture, honey, sugar, and vanilla extract. Stir until sugar dissolves.
3. **Chill**: Refrigerate the mixture for at least 4 hours or overnight.
4. **Churn**: Once chilled, churn the mixture in an ice cream maker according to the manufacturer's instructions. Freeze until firm.

Chocolate Marshmallow Ice Cream

Ingredients:

- 2 cups heavy cream
- 1 cup whole milk
- 1/2 cup sugar
- 1/2 cup cocoa powder
- 1 cup marshmallow fluff
- 1 tsp vanilla extract

Instructions:

1. **Make the base**: In a bowl, whisk together heavy cream, whole milk, sugar, cocoa powder, and vanilla extract until smooth.
2. **Chill**: Refrigerate the mixture for at least 4 hours or overnight.
3. **Churn**: Once chilled, churn the mixture in an ice cream maker according to the manufacturer's instructions.
4. **Add marshmallow fluff**: During the last few minutes of churning, swirl in the marshmallow fluff to create ribbons of marshmallow throughout the ice cream. Freeze until firm.

Orange Creamsicle Ice Cream

Ingredients:

- 2 cups heavy cream
- 1 cup whole milk
- 1/2 cup orange juice (freshly squeezed)
- 1 tbsp orange zest
- 1/2 cup sugar
- 1 tsp vanilla extract

Instructions:

1. **Make the base**: In a bowl, combine heavy cream, whole milk, orange juice, orange zest, sugar, and vanilla extract. Stir until the sugar is dissolved.
2. **Chill**: Refrigerate the mixture for at least 4 hours or overnight.
3. **Churn**: Once chilled, churn the mixture in an ice cream maker according to the manufacturer's instructions. Freeze until firm.

Banana Foster Ice Cream

Ingredients:

- 2 cups heavy cream
- 1 cup whole milk
- 3/4 cup brown sugar
- 1/2 cup dark rum
- 1 cup mashed ripe bananas
- 1 tsp vanilla extract

Instructions:

1. **Make the base**: In a saucepan, combine heavy cream, whole milk, and brown sugar. Heat over medium heat, stirring until the sugar is dissolved.
2. **Banana mixture**: In a bowl, combine the mashed bananas, dark rum, and vanilla extract. Stir into the cream mixture once it has cooled.
3. **Chill**: Refrigerate the mixture for at least 4 hours or overnight.
4. **Churn**: Once chilled, churn the mixture in an ice cream maker according to the manufacturer's instructions. Freeze until firm.

Mixed Berry Sorbet

Ingredients:

- 4 cups mixed berries (strawberries, raspberries, blueberries, etc.)
- 1/2 cup sugar
- 1/2 cup water
- 1 tbsp lemon juice

Instructions:

1. **Puree the berries**: In a blender or food processor, puree the mixed berries until smooth. Strain the mixture to remove the seeds if desired.
2. **Make the syrup**: In a saucepan, combine sugar and water. Heat over medium heat until sugar dissolves. Let cool.
3. **Combine**: Stir the berry puree and lemon juice into the cooled syrup.
4. **Churn**: Pour the mixture into an ice cream maker and churn according to the manufacturer's instructions. Freeze until firm.

Salted Chocolate Ice Cream

Ingredients:

- 2 cups heavy cream
- 1 cup whole milk
- 3/4 cup sugar
- 1/2 cup cocoa powder
- 1 tsp vanilla extract
- 1 tsp sea salt
- 1/2 cup dark chocolate, chopped

Instructions:

1. **Make the base**: In a bowl, whisk together heavy cream, whole milk, sugar, cocoa powder, and vanilla extract until smooth.
2. **Chill**: Refrigerate the mixture for at least 4 hours or overnight.
3. **Melt the chocolate**: In a microwave or over a double boiler, melt the dark chocolate. Stir the melted chocolate and sea salt into the chilled mixture.
4. **Churn**: Once chilled, churn the mixture in an ice cream maker according to the manufacturer's instructions. Freeze until firm.

www.ingramcontent.com/pod-product-compliance
Lightning Source LLC
LaVergne TN
LVHW061955070526
838199LV00060B/4128